OCT - - 2018

S0-AYU-683

Rectangles and Triangles
A song about Drawing with shapes

By BLAKE HOENA
Illustrations by TIM PALIN
Music by EMILY ARROW

Walpole Public Library
Walpole, Mass.

CANTATA
LEARNING

WWW.CANTATALEARNING.COM

J
Pic

- 344l764

CANTATA
LEARNING

Published by Cantata Learning
1710 Roe Crest Drive
North Mankato, MN 56003
www.cantatalearning.com

Copyright © 2018 Cantata Learning

All rights reserved. No part of this publication may be reproduced
in any form without written permission from the publisher.

Library of Congress Cataloging-in-Publication Data
Names: Hoena, B. A. | Palin, Tim, illustrator. | Arrow, Emily.
Title: Rectangles and triangles : a song about drawing with shapes / by Blake
    Hoena ; illustrations by Tim Palin ; music by Emily Arrow.
Description: North Mankato, MN : Cantata Learning, [2018] | Series: Sing and
    draw! | Audience: Age -8. | Audience: K to grade 3.
Identifiers: LCCN 2017007525 | ISBN 9781684100477 (hardcover : alk. paper)
Subjects: LCSH: Geometry, Plane--Juvenile literature. | Rectangles--Juvenile
    literature. | Triangle--Juvenile literature. | Shapes--Juvenile literature.
Classification: LCC QA482 .H64 2018 | DDC 516/.154--dc23
LC record available at https://lccn.loc.gov/2017007525

Book design, Tim Palin Creative
Editorial direction, Flat Sole Studio
Executive musical production and direction, Elizabeth Draper
Music arranged and produced by Emily Arrow

Printed in the United States of America in North Mankato, Minnesota.
072017   0367CGF17

ACCESS THE MUSIC!

SCAN
CODE
WITH
MOBILE
APP

CANTATALEARNING.COM

TIPS TO SUPPORT LITERACY AT HOME

WHY READING AND SINGING WITH YOUR CHILD IS SO IMPORTANT

Daily reading with your child leads to increased academic achievement. Music and songs, specifically rhyming songs, are a fun and easy way to build early literacy and language development. Music skills correlate significantly with both phonological awareness and reading development. Singing helps build vocabulary and speech development. And reading and appreciating music together is a wonderful way to strengthen your relationship.

READ AND SING EVERY DAY!

TIPS FOR USING CANTATA LEARNING BOOKS AND SONGS DURING YOUR DAILY STORY TIME

1. As you sing and read, point out the different words on the page that rhyme. Suggest other words that rhyme.

2. Memorize simple rhymes such as Itsy Bitsy Spider and sing them together. This encourages comprehension skills and early literacy skills.

3. Use the questions in the back of each book to guide your singing and storytelling.

4. Read the included sheet music with your child while you listen to the song. How do the music notes correlate to the words of the song?

5. Sing along on the go and at home. Access music by scanning the QR code on each Cantata book. You can also stream or download the music for free to your computer, smartphone, or mobile device.

Devoting time to daily reading shows that you are available for your child. Together, you are building language, literacy, and listening skills.

Have fun reading and singing!

Do you like stories about princesses, knights, and dragons? Then grab your drawing supplies. You're going on a quest! You will use rectangles and triangles to learn how to draw an adventure story.

Now turn the page and get ready to draw. Remember to sing along!

First, you will need a castle,
so draw a big rectangle.

Then add one more on each side,
tall towers to touch the sky.

Draw half-circles for windows
and a sturdy gate to close.

Along the top, draw small squares.
They will add a little **flair**.

Rectangles have four sides.
Triangles have three.

Use these two shapes to draw
your very own story!

Rectangles have four sides.
Triangles have three.

Princesses, **knights**, and dragons—
Let's draw them. It's easy!

A princess lives in the castle.
So start with a triangle.

A half-circle forms her face
and shows off all of her grace.

Then draw a triangle dress.
She will look her very best.

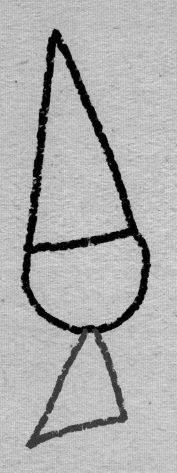

Lastly, add the small details:
hair, mouth, eyes, and a long **veil**.

Rectangles have four sides.
Triangles have three.

Use these two shapes to draw
your very own story!

Rectangles have four sides.
Triangles have three.

Princesses, knights, and dragons—
Let's draw them. It's easy!

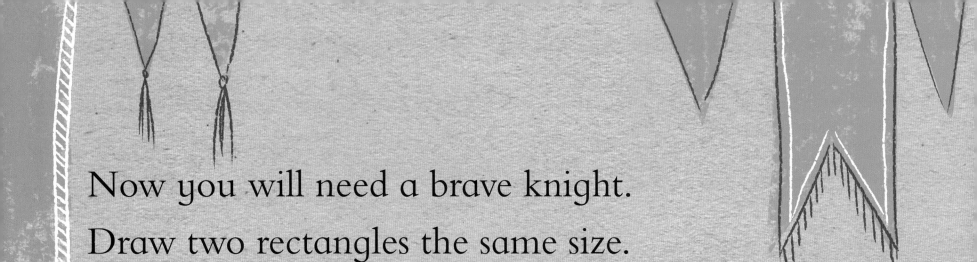

Now you will need a brave knight.

Draw two rectangles the same size.

Add a circle for his face.

Then draw one raised arm and legs.

Our knight will need a **weapon** to battle the mean dragon.

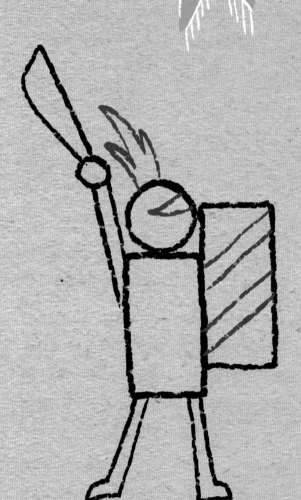

To his helm, add a **visor**.

Then decorate his **armor**.

Rectangles have four sides.
Triangles have three.

Use these two shapes to draw
your very own story!

Rectangles have four sides.
Triangles have three.

Princesses, knights, and dragons—
Let's draw them. It's easy!

The story needs a dragon.
A triangle starts the fun.

Draw two more for wings to **soar**
and two for a mouth to roar.

Then add a long, curvy tail
and arms and legs full of **scales**.

Small triangles form the spikes
down its back. Oh, what a fright!

Rectangles have four sides.
Triangles have three.

Use these two shapes to draw
your very own story!

Rectangles have four sides.
Triangles have three.

Princesses, knights, and dragons—
Let's draw them. It's easy!

SONG LYRICS
Rectangles and Squares

First, you will need a castle,
so draw a big rectangle.
Then, add one more on each side,
tall towers to touch the sky.
Draw half-circles for windows
and a sturdy gate to close.
Along the top, draw small squares.
They will add a little flair.

Rectangles have four sides.
Triangles have three.
Use these two shapes to draw
your very own story!

Rectangles have four sides.
Triangles have three.
Princesses, knights, and dragons—
Let's draw them. It's easy!

A princess lives in the castle.
So start with a triangle.
A half-circle forms her face
and shows off all of her grace.
Then draw a triangle dress.
She will look her very best.
Lastly, add the small details:
hair, mouth, eyes, and a long veil.

CHORUS
Rectangles have four sides.
Triangles have three.
Use these two shapes to draw
your very own story!

Rectangles have four sides.
Triangles have three.
Princesses, knights, and dragons—
Let's draw them. It's easy!

Now you will need a brave knight.
Draw two rectangles the same size.
Add a circle for his face.
Then draw one raised arm and legs.
Our knight will need a weapon
to battle the mean dragon.
To his helm, add a visor.
Then decorate his armor.

Rectangles have four sides.
Triangles have three.
Use these two shapes to draw
your very own story!

Rectangles have four sides.
Triangles have three.
Princesses, knights, and dragons—
Let's draw them. It's easy!

The story needs a dragon.
A triangle starts the fun.
Draw two more for wings to soar
and two for a mouth to roar.
Then add a long, curvy tail
and arms and legs full of scales.
Small triangles form the spikes
down its back. Oh, what a fright!

Rectangles have four sides.
Triangles have three.
Use these two shapes to draw
your very own story!

Rectangles have four sides.
Triangles have three.
Princesses, knights, and dragons—
Let's draw them. It's easy!

Rectangles and Triangles

Kindie
Emily Arrow

Verse

1. First, you will need a cas - tle, so draw a big rec - tan - gle. Then, add one more on each side, tall tow - ers to touch the sky. Draw half - cir - cles for win - dows and a stur - dy gate to close. A - long the top, draw small squares. They will add a lit - tle flair.

Chorus

Rec - tan - gles have four sides. Tri - an - gles have three. Use these two shapes to draw your ver - y own sto - ry! Rec - tan - gles have four sides. Tri - an - gles have three. Prin - cess - es, knights, and drag - ons — Let's draw them. It's eas - y!

Verse 2
A princess lives in the castle.
So start with a triangle.
A half-circle forms her face
and shows off all of her grace.
Then draw a triangle dress.
She will look her very best.
Lastly, add the small details:
hair, mouth, eyes, and a long veil.

Chorus

Verse 3
Now you will need a brave knight.
Draw two rectangles the same size.
Add a circle for his face.
Then draw one raised arm and legs.
Our knight will need a weapon
to battle the mean dragon.
To his helm, add a visor.
Then decorate his armor.

Chorus

Verse 4
The story needs a dragon.
A triangle starts the fun.
Draw two more for wings to soar
and two for a mouth to roar.
Then add a long, curvy tail
and arms and legs full of scales.
Small triangles form the spikes
down its back. Oh, what a fright!

Chorus

ACCESS THE MUSIC!
SCAN CODE WITH MOBILE APP
CANTATALEARNING.COM

GLOSSARY

armor—protective covering

flair—style

knight—a warrior who wore armor and often fought on horseback

scales—small, hard plates of skin that cover the bodies of reptiles and most fish

soar—to fly high in the air

veil—a piece of cloth worn as a covering for the head or face

visor—a covering, often attached to a hat or helmet, designed to shade the eyes

weapon—a tool used for fighting

GUIDED READING ACTIVITIES

1. Would you like to have a dragon as a pet? If yes, list three things you and your pet dragon could do together.

2. In this book, you learned how to draw a castle, princess, knight, and dragon. Draw a scene showing all four of these things.

3. Tell a story with you as the hero. Are you a princess or knight? Or a dragon? What adventures do you go on?

TO LEARN MORE

Harpster, Steve. *Drawing Dragons with Numbers*. Loudonville, OH: Harptoons Publishing, 2014.

Heos, Bridget. *Who Wants to Be a Princess?: What It Was Really Like to Be A Medieval Princess*. New York: Henry Holt and Company, 2017.

Lee, Sally. *Knights*. North Mankato, MN: Capstone, 2013.

Storey, Rita. *Knights and Castles*. Mankato, MN: Smart Apple Media, 2014.